SCHOLASTIC

READING
SATs TESTS
YEAR 4

SCHOLASTIC

Scholastic Education, an imprint of Scholastic Ltd
Book End, Range Road, Witney, Oxfordshire, OX29 0YD
Registered office: Westfield Road, Southam,
Warwickshire CV47 0RA
www.scholastic.co.uk

© 2019 Scholastic Ltd

1 2 3 4 5 6 7 8 9   9 0 1 2 3 4 5 6 7 8

A British Library Cataloguing-in-Publication Data
A catalogue record for this book is available from the British
Library.

ISBN 978-1407-18305-3
Printed and bound by Ashford Colour Press

Author
Catherine Casey

Series consultants
Lesley and Graham Fletcher

Editorial team
Rachel Morgan, Tracey Cowell, Anna Hall,
Maggie Donovan, Shelley Welsh and Helen Lewis

Design team
Nicolle Thomas and Oxford Designers and Illustrators

Cover illustrations
Istock/calvindexter and Tomek.gr / Shutterstock/Visual Generation

Acknowledgements
Extracts from Department for Education website © Crown Copyright. Reproduced under the terms of the Open Government Licence
(OGL). www.nationalarchives.gov.uk/doc/open-government-licence/version/3/

The publishers gratefully acknowledge permission to reproduce the following copyright material:
Catherine Casey for the use of 'To Mars', 'Beautiful birds', 'How to make a bird cake', 'The lion and the mouse: A fable', 'The lion', the
adaptation of 'Little Red Riding Hood', 'Volcanoes', 'Mary the evacuee', 'Cleaning your teeth', 'Vegetable pasta bake', 'All about your
teeth' and 'The duck rescue'. Text © 2015, Catherine Casey.
Every effort has been made to trace copyright holders for the works reproduced in this publication, and the publishers apologise for
any inadvertent omissions.

Illustrations: Moreno Chiacchiera, Beehive Illustration
Photographs:
Test A: © NikoNomad/Shutterstock; © TSpider/Shutterstock; © Danai Jetawattana/Shutterstock; © Marlee/Shutterstock;
    © David Soanes/Shutterstock; © Furtseff/Shutterstock; © Hfuchs/Shutterstock; © Timothy J Parry/Shutterstock;
    © Aleksey Karpenko/Shutterstock; © Eric Isselee/Shutterstock; © Allan W/Shutterstock.
Test B: © The Len/Shutterstock; © Ermolaev Alexander/Shutterstock; © Ruth Black/Shutterstock; © Fotos593/Shutterstock;
    © Corbac40/Shutterstock; © drli/Shutterstock; © TopFoto.
Test C: © Veronica Louro/Shutterstock; © Anna Bogush/Shutterstock; © Andi Berger/Shutterstock; © Elena Veselova/Shutterstock;
    © Jovanovic Dejan/Shutterstock; © Blue Sky Image/Shutterstock; © Paul Burns/Shutterstock.

Contents
Reading Year 4

Contents	Page
Introduction	
About this book	4
Advice for parents and carers	5
Advice for children	6
Test coverage	6
Tests	
Test A	7
Test B	28
Test C	49
Marks & guidance	
Marking and assessing the papers	70
Mark scheme for Test A	71
Mark scheme for Test B	73
Mark scheme for Test C	76

About this book

This book provides you with practice papers to help support children with end-of-year tests and to assess which skills need further development.

Using the practice papers

The practice papers in this book can be used as you would any other practice materials. The children will need to be familiar with specific test-focused skills, such as reading carefully, leaving questions until the end if they seem too difficult, working at a suitable pace and checking through their work.

If you choose to use the papers for looking at content rather than practising tests, do be aware of the time factor. The tests require a lot of work to be done in 1 hour as they are testing the degree of competence children have – it is not enough to be able to answer questions correctly but slowly.

About the tests

Each Reading test consists of texts covering different genres and contains 50 marks. Each test lasts for 1 hour, including reading time.

- Reading texts: children may underline, highlight or make notes.
- Questions: children should refer back to the reading texts for their answers.

The marks available for each question are shown in the test paper next to each question and are also shown next to each answer in the mark scheme. Incorrect answers do not get a mark and no half marks should be given.

There are three different types of answer.

- **Selected answers**: children may be required to choose an option from a list; draw lines to match answers; or tick a correct answer. Usually 1 mark will be awarded.
- **Short answers**: children will need to write a phrase or use information from the text. Usually 1–2 marks will be awarded.
- **Several line answers**: children will need to write a sentence or two. Usually 1–2 marks will be awarded.
- **Longer answers**: children will usually need to write more than one sentence using information from the text. Up to 3 marks will be awarded.

Advice for parents and carers

How this book will help

This book will support your child to get ready for the school-based end-of-year tests in Reading. It provides valuable practice and help on the responses and content expected of Year 4 children aged 8–9 years.

In the weeks leading up to the school tests, your child will be given plenty of practice, revision and tips to give them the best possible chance to demonstrate their knowledge and understanding. It is important to try to practise outside of school, and many children benefit from extra input. This book will help your child prepare and build their confidence and ability to work to a time limit. Practice is vital and every opportunity helps, so don't start too late.

In this book you will find three Reading tests. The layout and format of each test closely matches those used in the National Tests, so your child will become familiar with what to expect and get used to the style of the tests. There is a comprehensive answer section and guidance about how to mark the questions.

Tips

- Make sure that you allow your child to take the tests in a quiet environment where they are not likely to be interrupted or distracted.
- Make sure your child has a flat surface to work on with plenty of space to spread out and good light.
- Emphasise the importance of reading and re-reading a question and to underline or circle any important information.
- These tests are similar to the ones your child will take in May in Year 6 and they therefore give you a good idea of strengths and areas for development. So, when you have found areas that require some more practice, it is useful to go over these again and practise similar types of questions with your child.
- Go through the tests again together, identify any gaps in learning and address any misconceptions or areas of misunderstanding. If you are unsure of anything yourself, then make an appointment to see your child's teacher who will be able to help and advise further.

Advice for children

What to do before the test

- Revise and practise on a regular basis.
- Spend some time each week practising.
- Focus on the areas you are least confident in to get better.
- Get a good night's sleep and eat a wholesome breakfast.
- Be on time for school.
- Have all the necessary materials.
- Avoid stressful situations before a test.

What to do in the test

- The test is 60 minutes long. You should allow time to read the texts and then answer the questions.
- Read one text and then answer the questions about that text before moving on to read the next text.
- You may highlight, underline or make notes on the texts.
- There are 50 marks. The marks for each question are shown in the margin on the right of each page.
- Make sure you read the instructions carefully. There are different types of answer.
  - Short answers: have a short line or box. This shows that you need only write a word or a few words in your answer.
  - Several line answers: have a few lines. This gives you space to write more words or a sentence or two.
  - Longer answers: have lots of lines. This shows that a longer, more detailed answer is needed. You can write in full sentences if you want to.
  - Selected answers: for these questions, you do not need to write anything at all and you should tick, draw lines to, or put a ring around your answer. Read the instructions carefully so that you know how to answer the question.

Test coverage

Children will need to be able to:

- Give and explain meanings of words.
- Find and copy key details.
- Summarise main ideas from more than one paragraph.
- Use details from the texts to explain their thoughts about them.
- Predict what might happen.
- Identify and explain how information is organised.
- Show how writers use language to create an effect.

Test A

To Mars

Zooming up into space,
Moving at a lightning pace.
A satellite sent out to Mars,
Into the universe with the stars.

Into orbit, round and round,
Scientists wait to see what's found.
Digital photographs it will take,
Such a long journey it has to make.

Investigating the planet red,
So many questions in my head.
It looks so red because of rust,
And storms can cause great clouds of dust.

The planet Mars is so very cold,
Minus temperatures so I'm told.
A satellite sent to find out more,
To answer questions and explore.

BEAUTIFUL BIRDS

There are many different types of bird living in the cities, towns and countryside around Britain. Some birds live in Britain all year round while others migrate to warmer countries in the winter. Have you ever stopped to listen to their beautiful song and watch them at the park or in a garden? You can learn a lot about birds this way, and it can be very relaxing to watch and listen.

Watching birds

You can encourage birds by making sure they have something to eat and somewhere suitable to nest. You have to be very quiet when bird watching so you don't scare all the birds away. You don't need any special equipment, but binoculars can help you to see the birds more clearly. Some bird watchers also hide or camouflage themselves among the natural surroundings so the birds don't see them.

Which birds will *you* be able to spot? You could keep a chart of the different types of bird and how many of each you see. Why not have a bird-spotting competition with your friends?

Did you know?

- Pigeons can be trained to carry messages. During the Second World War, thousands of pigeons were used by the army to carry messages.

- Magpies were believed to like shiny things and often steal them for their nests, but more recent research shows that this is not true.

- Some people believe that seeing a magpie can bring you good or bad luck depending on how many there are. You may know the old nursery rhyme: 'One for sorrow, Two for joy…'

Take a look at the fact files below and see if you can spot any of these birds when you are out and about.

Robin

Appearance

Robins have a distinctive red chest and brown feathers on their wings.

Food

They eat worms from the ground.

Where to find them

British robins are often found in gardens, usually alone.

Pigeon

Appearance

Pigeons are grey with small heads. They can be quite large.

Food

They eat seeds and berries.

Where to find them

Pigeons are often found in cities and towns.

Blue tit

Appearance

Blue tits are little birds with a beautiful yellow chest and bright blue feathers on their wings.

Food

They eat juicy caterpillars, nuts and seeds.

Where to find them

Blue tits are usually found up in the trees.

Sparrow

Appearance

Sparrows have black faces and black and brown wings.

Food

They eat seeds and nuts.

Where to find them

Sparrows like to live near people and buildings. So towns, cities and housing estates are good places to look for sparrows.

Blackbird

Appearance

Only male blackbirds are black. The females are actually brown!

Food

They eat wriggly worms from the ground.

Where to find them

Blackbirds are often found in gardens and parks, usually looking for worms.

Magpie

Appearance

Magpies are quite large birds. They have a black head, chest and wings with a white tummy. They have a long black tail.

Food

They eat a wide range of things including insects, berries, seeds and even eggs.

Where to find them

Magpies can be found in gardens and parks.

How to make a bird cake

Encourage birds to your garden or school grounds by providing them with food in the winter when it is difficult for them to find their own food. This will help you to learn more about wildlife, while the birds help to protect and maintain your garden by eating seeds and insects.

You will need:

- clean empty yoghurt pot
- piece of string
- scissors
- knife
- 400g of lard, at room temperature
- 300g of bird seeds, bird nuts, currants, bread crumbs/plain biscuits
- large bowl

These wonderful bird cakes are quick and easy to make. Simply hang them in a good spot, then watch and wait for the hungry birds to come.

What to do

1 Carefully, pierce a hole in the bottom of the empty yoghurt pot.

2 Thread the piece of string through the hole and pull all the way through the yoghurt pot.

3 Cut the lard into small cubes, using the knife.

4 In a large bowl, mix the lard, bird seeds, bird nuts, currants, bread crumbs/plain biscuits together, using your hands. (This is messy but fun!)

5 Fill the yoghurt pot with the sticky mixture. Press it down firmly and make sure the string is threaded all the way through the middle of the mixture.

6 Put the filled yoghurt pot into the fridge for at least three hours to set.

7 Once the mixture is hard, remove the yoghurt pot. (It doesn't matter if you need to break the pot.)

8 Hang your bird cake in a tree or bush, using the string to tie it onto a branch.

9 Enjoy watching the birds as they peck at your tasty bird cake, but remember to stay quiet so you don't scare them.

10 When the birds have eaten the bird cake you can make another one!

Important points!

- Don't add anything to your bird cake that contains salt (such as salted nuts) as this will make the birds ill.
- Bird seeds and bird nuts are not suitable for humans so don't be tempted to try your creation. It's just for the birds!

The lion and the mouse: A fable

One hot sunny day, a large, lazy lion lay asleep in the shade of a tree. The hot sun beamed down but there was a gentle breeze in the air. Other animals in the forest were busy and hard at work. The bees were buzzing around making honey. The noise of buzzing irritated the snoozing lion and he angrily swished his tail at the bees. An army of ants marched in a line, carrying food back to their nest. As they climbed over the lion's back, they tickled him and disturbed him from his nap. This made the lion really cross, so he shook and wriggled until the ants fell off. Then, just as the sleepy lion settled back down and closed his eyes, a poor little mouse, scuttling home, crashed straight into him.

Now the lion had definitely had enough! He was furious. All he wanted was to sleep in the afternoon sunshine. Was that too much to ask? He snatched up the mouse in his paw and held her tight in his claws. The lion let out an enormous roar, and his sharp pointy teeth glistened in the sunlight. The little creature trembled in the lion's grip and a tiny tear rolled down her cheek. Her long whiskers quivered in fear.

"Please don't eat me," the mouse whispered.

"Why not?" the lion bellowed. He peered over his huge wet nose to look closely at the little mouse. "Do tell me, please," the lion asked.

"If you let me go I will remember your kindness and one day I will be able to help you in return," replied the little mouse.

To the mouse's surprise the lion laughed and chuckled and giggled to himself. His thick furry mane bounced around but he still gripped the mouse firmly in his paw.

"A tiny little mouse like you could never help a big powerful lion like me, but because you are so funny I will let you go," said the lion, putting the mouse down on the ground carefully and setting her free.

Although she disagreed, the clever mouse did not stop to argue, and she ran home. For a time, the lion thought the idea that a little mouse could help him was so funny that he kept telling all the other animals in the forest about it. But as the weeks passed, the lion forgot all about the little mouse who had accidentally run into him. She did not forget him, though.

Many months later, the little mouse was clearing the path of leaves when she heard the enormous roar of the large, lazy lion. Bravely, she ran to see if he needed help. The lion lay tangled and trapped in a hunter's net. He had been captured. The little mouse set to work. She nibbled and nibbled at the thick heavy ropes until, finally, the lion was set free.

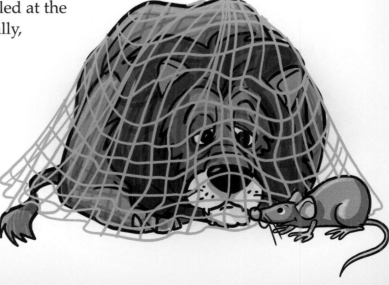

"You see," said the little mouse, "even a creature as small as me can help a creature as big as you." Then, with a big smile across her face, she quickly scampered away. The lion had learned a very important lesson.

> **Questions** 1–6 are about *To Mars* on page **8**.

1. What are the main ideas of the poem?

Tick **two**.

A satellite is going to Mars. ☐

Nobody lives on Mars. ☐

There are aliens on Mars. ☐

The satellite will explore the surface of Mars. ☐

The satellite will tell the weather on Mars. ☐

2

2. Who is waiting to see what the satellite finds?

_____

1

3. What type of photographs will the satellite take?

_____

1

Marks

4. What colour does the text say the planet Mars is and what does it suggest the cause of this colour is?

Colour: _____

Cause: _____

2

5. Which word in the text rhymes with *explore*?

_____

1

6. Why has a satellite been sent to Mars? Give **two** reasons.

1. _____

2. _____

2

Test A

Questions 7–19 are about *Beautiful birds* on pages **9–10**.

7.

*...others **migrate** to warmer countries in the winter.*

What does the word *migrate* mean?

Tick **one**.

Journey ☐

Live in ☐

Dislike ☐

Prefer ☐

1

8.

*...somewhere **suitable** to nest.*

What does the word *suitable* mean?

_____

1

Marks

9. Why do you have to be quiet when you are bird watching?

_____

_____

1

10. Why are binoculars useful when you are bird watching?

_____

_____

1

11. Why do some bird watchers camouflage themselves?

_____

_____

1

12. How could you keep track of the birds that you see?
Circle **one**.

hide in camouflage   keep a chart

be quiet   migrate

1

13. Which birds were used by the army in the Second World War?

_____

_____

Marks

1

14. According to the nursery rhyme, how many magpies bring joy?

_____

_____

1

15. Which bird has bright blue feathers on its wings?
Circle **one**.

| Robin | Blue tit | Magpie | Sparrow |

_____

1

16. Which bird is usually found alone?

Tick **one**.

Pigeon ☐

Sparrow ☐

Blackbird ☐

Robin ☐

1

SCHOLASTIC National Curriculum SATs Tests

17. What colour are female blackbirds?

_____

_____

18. What do sparrows eat?

_____

_____

19. Draw lines to match the birds to their habitat.

Bird	**Habitat**
Blackbirds	In the trees
Blue tits	Towns and cities
Sparrows	Gardens and parks

Marks

1

1

1

| | Marks |

Questions 20–27 are about *How to make a bird cake* on page 11.

20. Why is it difficult for birds to find their own food in winter?

_____

_____

1

21. Which of the following do you need to make a bird cake?

Tick **one**.

A piece of string ☐

Tin can ☐

Flour ☐

Eggs ☐

1

22. How many grams (g) of lard do you need?

_____

1

Marks

23.

> These **wonderful** bird cakes are quick and easy to make.

Why has the author used the word *wonderful*?

Tick **one**.

They are difficult to make. ☐

To encourage the reader to make a bird cake. ☐

They look pretty. ☐

They are delicious for humans to eat. ☐

1

24.

> Carefully, pierce a hole in the bottom of the empty yoghurt pot.

a. What does the word *pierce* mean?

_____

1

b. What does the word *carefully* mean in this sentence? Explain why you must be careful.

_____

_____

2

25. Where should you hang your bird cake?

_____

_____

1

26. a. What type of nuts should you NOT add to the bird cake?

_____

1

b. Why?

Tick **one**.

They would not taste very nice. ⬜

They would make the lard melt. ⬜

They would not look very good. ⬜

They would make the birds ill. ⬜

1

27. Who is the bird cake NOT for?

_____

1

Marks

Questions 28–39 are about *The lion and the mouse: A fable* on pages **12–13**.

28.

a large, lazy lion lay asleep

What does this tell you about the lion?

Tick **one**.

He is brave. ☐

His is hard at work. ☐

He is idle. ☐

He is trapped. ☐

1

29. Where was the lion lying asleep?

_____

1

Marks

30. What were the ants carrying?

_____

1

31. How do you think the mouse felt when she was captured? Give **three** pieces of evidence from the text to explain your answer.

_____

_____

_____

_____

3

32.

"Why not?" the lion **bellowed**.

What does _bellowed_ mean?

_____

1

33. Why did the lion let the mouse go?

_____

1

SCHOLASTIC National Curriculum SATs Tests

34. Explain why the mouse didn't argue with the lion even though she disagreed with him.

_____

_____

Marks

2

35. What was the mouse doing later when she heard the lion roar for help?

_____

1

36. Explain why the mouse was brave to go and help the lion. Give **two** pieces of evidence from the text to explain your answer.

_____

_____

2

37. | *The lion lay tangled... in a hunter's net.* |

How do you think the lion felt when he was trapped?

_____

_____

1

38. Explain why the mouse had a big smile on her face after she had helped the lion. Give **two** pieces of evidence from the text to explain your answer.

_____

_____

2

39. What lesson did the lion learn?

_____

1

End of test

Question	Focus	Possible marks	Actual marks
1	Summarise	2	
2	Information/key details	1	
3	Information/key details	1	
4	Information/key details / Making inferences	2	
5	Identifying/explaining choice of words and phrases	1	
6	Information/key details	2	
7	Meaning of words	1	
8	Meaning of words	1	
9	Information/key details	1	
10	Information/key details	1	
11	Information/key details	1	
12	Information/key details	1	
13	Information/key details	1	
14	Information/key details	1	
15	Information/key details	1	
16	Information/key details	1	
17	Information/key details	1	
18	Information/key details	1	
19	Information/key details	1	
20	Making inferences	1	
21	Information/key details	1	
22	Information/key details	1	
23	Identifying/explaining choice of words and phrases	1	
24	Meaning of words	3	
25	Information/key details	1	
26	Information/key details	2	
27	Information/key details	1	
28	Identifying/explaining choice of words and phrases	1	
29	Identifying/explaining choice of words and phrases	1	
30	Information/key details	1	
31	Making inferences	3	
32	Meaning of words	1	
33	Making inferences	1	
34	Making inferences	2	
35	Information/key details	1	
36	Making inferences	2	
37	Making inferences	1	
38	Making inferences	2	
39	Making inferences	1	
	Total	50	

Test B

The lion

Prowling up and down the fence,
Visitors watching, looking tense.
His legs and paws so very strong,
His swishing tail so very long.

When it's feeding time at the zoo,
The fearsome lioness is there too.
Watch them pounce on the red, raw meat,
A tasty feast for them to eat.

See the lion stretch those knife-sharp claws,
Stamping down his powerful paws.
Look at those teeth as he opens his jaw,
Cover your ears when he lets out a roar.

See his piercing bright yellow eyes,
Staring up at the annoying flies.
The fluffy mane shakes around his head,
As he settles down now, sleepy and well fed.

There is no doubt just who is in charge,
This magnificent lion, so very large.

Little Red Riding Hood

Cast:

Little Red Riding Hood
Mother
Big Bad Wolf
Grandma
Woodcutter

Scene 1: Little Red Riding Hood's house

Little Red Riding Hood is sitting on the floor playing with her toy dolly. Mother is standing at the kitchen table packing a basket with small cakes and fruit.

Mother:	Little Red Riding Hood, could you take this basket of fruit and cakes to Grandma please?
Little Red Riding Hood:	Yes, Mother, of course. I love visiting Grandma. Ooo these cakes smell delicious. (*coming over to the table*)
Mother:	Put on your coat. It's cold out. Make sure you stay on the path at all times and don't speak to any strangers. (*looking worried*)
Little Red Riding Hood:	Yes, Mother. (*putting on her red coat and pulling up her hood*)
Mother:	Be as quick as you can now. (*looking worried again*)
Little Red Riding Hood:	Bye, Mother. (*skipping out of the door with the basket of fruit and cakes over her arm*)

Scene 2: The woods — with a stone path in the middle, surrounded by bluebells and tall trees on either side

Little Red Riding Hood is skipping down the path carrying the basket of fruit and cakes.

Little Red Riding Hood:	(*stopping and pointing*) Look at those beautiful bright bluebells. A lovely bunch of those would cheer Grandma up. (*walking off the path into the woods to pick bluebells*)
Big Bad Wolf:	(*popping out from behind a tree*) Hello. Those are beautiful flowers you're picking.
Little Red Riding Hood:	Oh, hello. Yes, they're for my grandma. She's poorly. I thought they would cheer her up.
Big Bad Wolf:	Oh, what a sweetheart you are. Let me help you. (*starting to pick flowers*)
Little Red Riding Hood:	Thank you. That's very kind. Now I must be going. Grandma will be wondering where I am.
Big Bad Wolf:	Where does your Grandma live, little girl? Is it far?

Little Red Riding Hood:	No, not much further. The little yellow cottage in the middle of the wood. Bye. Thank you for your help picking the flowers. (*skipping off down the path*)
Big Bad Wolf:	(*rubbing his hands together and licking his lips*) Lucky for me no-one told that silly girl to stay on the path and not talk to strangers! I am going to have a delicious, tasty lunch today. If I am quick I can get to Grandma's before the girl. (*running off into the woods*)

Scene 3: Grandma's house — the little yellow cottage in the woods

Grandma is locked in the cupboard. The Big Bad Wolf is sitting in Grandma's rocking chair wearing her shawl, hat and glasses. Little Red Riding Hood knocks on the door.

Big Bad Wolf:	Come in, little grandchild. The door is open.
Little Red Riding Hood:	Oh, Grandma. You look very poorly.
Big Bad Wolf:	Oh, I'm not that bad. (*grinning and peering over his glasses*)
Little Red Riding Hood:	What big eyes you've got.
Big Bad Wolf:	All the better to see you with.
Little Red Riding Hood:	What big ears you've got, Grandma.
Big Bad Wolf:	All the better to hear you with.
Little Red Riding Hood:	And Grandma, what big teeth you've got!
Big Bad Wolf:	(*throwing off his disguise*) All the better to eat you with!
Little Red Riding Hood:	Help! HELP! HELP! (*Little Red Riding Hood runs around the stage with the Big Bad Wolf chasing her*)
Woodcutter:	(*bursting through the door*) Stop right there, Mr Big Bad Wolf!
Big Bad Wolf:	Oh, why did you have to spoil everything? (*walks out of the door, sulking*)
Little Red Riding Hood:	Thank you, Mr Woodcutter. I'm sorry I left the path and spoke to a stranger. I won't do it again, I promise.
Grandma:	Let me out! Let me out! (*knocking on the cupboard door*)
Woodcutter:	Oh, Grandma, are you all right? (*unlocking the cupboard door and helping Grandma out*)
Little Red Riding Hood:	Grandma! (*hugging Grandma*) I brought you a basket of cakes and fruit.
Grandma:	Thank you dear! Let's put the kettle on and make a nice cup of tea for everyone. Mr Woodcutter, would you stay for tea and cake?
Woodcutter:	Yes, please. Those cakes do smell delicious!

Volcanoes

There are thousands of volcanoes around the world. Most volcanoes are along the Earth's plate edges, some of which are under the sea. Find out here what a volcano is, the effects of an explosion and why some people still live near volcanoes.

What is a volcano?

A volcano is a place where magma and molten rock explode through the Earth's surface. A mountain is often created during the process. Magma from deep inside the Earth's core erupts and red lava flows over the Earth's surface. The very hot temperatures mean that it destroys anything in its path.

Types of volcano

There are three main types of volcano:

1. Active volcanoes

These are volcanoes that have erupted within the last 10,000 years.

2. Dormant volcanoes

These are volcanoes that have not erupted within the last 10,000 years, but scientists believe they could erupt again.

3. Extinct volcanoes

These are volcanoes that have not erupted within the last 10,000 years, and scientists think it is unlikely they will ever erupt again.

A volcano erupting

volcanic ash

lava

magma

Effects of a volcanic eruption

The effects of a volcano exploding can be devastating! The moving lava and hot volcanic ash can destroy homes and businesses, kill people and wipe out whole villages, towns and even cities.

Mount Vesuvius overlooks the Bay of Naples.

Why do people live near volcanoes?

Despite the dangers, many people still live near active volcanoes. There are even large cities near some of the world's active volcanoes. This is mainly because the soil is so rich and therefore crops grow extremely well. Volcanoes also attract tourists who want to see a volcano, and this can provide jobs for those living nearby.

Key words

Word	Meaning
Magma	Magma is molten rock from deep inside the Earth.
Lava	Lava is magma that has erupted from the volcano. It is a red-hot flowing liquid.
Volcanic ash	Volcanic ash is made up of tiny pieces of rocks and minerals thrown from the volcano in an eruption.
Molten rock	Molten rock is rock that has got so hot it has melted and formed a liquid.
Earth's plates	The Earth's surface is made up of several plates that fit together like a puzzle.
Earth's core	The Earth's core is the centre of the Earth.
Erupt	When something erupts it explodes or bursts out.

Mary the evacuee

It was 1940 and the Second World War had started. Bombs were falling on London and many children were being evacuated to the countryside to keep them safe.

Mary was cold, standing on the platform waiting for the train. She held on tight to her small brown suitcase with both hands. Just like all the other children being evacuated, Mary had a brown cardboard label with her name on around her neck. She was dressed in her best clothes ('to make a good first impression,' her mother had said): a pretty blue dress that her mother had made her, a cardigan and polished brown shoes. The platform was busy, full of small children in their best clothes and mothers with hankies to wipe their tears away. Some of the other children were with their brothers and sisters but Mary only had one brother, who was much older than her and had gone away to war with the men.

Mary felt frightened. She hadn't been to the countryside before and she would miss her mother. But she was a little excited, too. She had heard of cows and sheep and seen them in books, but never any real ones. Mary wondered what it would be like out in the country and in her new home.

As the train steamed into the railway station, it hissed before coming to a stop. Mary waved to her mother, who was drying her tears and trying to look brave, and she climbed aboard. Hundreds of children piled in together. Mary sat next to another girl who was a bit older than her. She was on her own too and was crying. Mary gave her a hanky to dry her eyes and they both waved out of the window as the train set off. Clickity clack, clickity clack. The train wobbled from side to side.

It was a long journey. Mary and the older girl, whose name was Janet, watched out of the grubby, draughty window. They saw the buildings, roads and bridges disappear and green fields and trees come into view. They smiled when they saw *real* cows in a field for the first time! It had been a grey cold day when they left London but the countryside seemed brighter and full of colour. The two girls had talked non-stop on the journey, and by the time they arrived in the country they were firm friends. They held hands as they were taken into the little village hall and hoped they would be able to stay together…

Marks

Questions 1–8 are about *The lion* on page **29**.

1. In the poem, what are the visitors doing?

_____

_____

1

2. Which word rhymes with *fence*?

_____

_____

1

3. Where is the lion?

_____

_____

1

4. Which word does the author use to describe:

a. the lion's claws?

_____

1

b. the lion's paws?

_____

1

5. Why do you think the author says to cover your ears when the lion roars?

_____

_____

6. Why do you think the lion might find the flies annoying?

_____

_____

7.

> This **magnificent** lion, so very large.

What does the word _magnificent_ mean?

_____

_____

8. What effect does rhyming have on the text?

_____

Marks

1

1

1

1

Marks

Questions 9–20 are about *Little Red Riding Hood* on pages **30–31**.

9. Where is Little Red Riding Hood going?

_____

_____

1

10. Why does Little Red Riding Hood leave the path?

_____

_____

1

11.

> **Big Bad Wolf:** (rubbing his hands together and licking his lips) Lucky for me no-one told that silly girl...

Why does the Big Bad Wolf rub his hands and lick his lips?

_____

1

Marks

12.

> **Big Bad Wolf:** (throwing off his **disguise**) All the better to eat you with!

What does the word *disguise* mean in this example?

Tick one.

Little Red Riding Hood's cloak ☐

Grandma's blanket ☐

The woodcutter's axe ☐

Grandma's clothes ☐

1

13.

> **Little Red Riding Hood:** Help! HELP! HELP! (Little Red Riding Hood runs around the stage...)

Why is the word *HELP* written in capital letters?

_____

_____

1

14. Who is the hero in this story?

_____

1

15. Number these events (1–5) to show the order in which they take place. The first one has been done for you.

	Marks
The woodcutter rescues Little Red Riding Hood from the Big Bad Wolf.	
The Big Bad Wolf talks to Little Red Riding Hood in the woods.	
The Big Bad Wolf dresses in Grandma's clothes.	
Little Red Riding Hood is asked to take a basket of cakes and fruit to Grandma's house.	I
Little Red Riding Hood leaves the path to pick bluebells.	

1

16. Fill in the boxes a–c with the following words and phrases to label the highlighted features of the text. One has been done for you.

Marks

| dialogue | cast member | stage directions |

a.

↓

Big Bad Wolf: (*popping out from behind a tree*) Hello. Those are beautiful flowers you're picking.

b. cast member

↓

Little Red Riding Hood: Oh, hello. Yes, they're for my grandma. She's poorly. I thought they would cheer her up.

c.

↓

Big Bad Wolf: Oh what a sweetheart you are. Let me help you. (*starting to pick flowers*)

1

17. What is the purpose of stage directions?

Tick **one**.

To tell the actors what to say ☐

To tell the actors what to do ☐

To tell the audience what is happening ☐

To tell the cast who is speaking ☐

1

18. What do you think the woodcutter, Grandma and Little Red Riding Hood do next? Explain why, giving **one** reason from the text.

_____

_____

Marks

2

19. How does the reader know that Little Red Riding Hood likes her grandma? Use evidence from the text to explain your answer. Give **two** reasons.

1. _____

_____

2. _____

_____

2

20. Describe the personality of Little Red Riding Hood. Give **three** pieces of evidence from the text to explain your answer.

_____

_____

_____

3

> **Questions** 21–30 are about *Volcanoes* on pages **32–33**.

21. In the text, where are most of the world's volcanoes?

Tick **one**.

In the USA ☐

Along the Earth's plate edges ☐

Under the sea ☐

In Europe ☐

1

22.

> *magma and molten rock* **explode** *through the earth's surface.*

Explain what the word *explode* means in this sentence.

_____

1

23.

> *A mountain is often created during the process.*

How do you think a mountain is created?

_____

1

24. How many main types of volcano are there?

_____

_____

Marks

1

25. What is a dormant volcano?

_____

_____

_____

1

26.

> *The effects of a volcanic explosion can be **devastating**!*

What does the word *devastating* mean?

_____

_____

1

27. Give **two** reasons from the text to explain why people still live near volcanoes, despite the risks.

1. _____

2. _____

2

28. What is magma?

_____

_____

1

29. What is volcanic ash?

_____

_____

1

30.

> _Earth's plates: The Earth's surface is made up of several plates that fit together **like a puzzle**._

How does the phrase _like a puzzle_ help you to understand what the Earth's plates are?

Tick one.

It helps us to visualise them as a game. ☐

It helps us to visualise them as being tiny. ☐

It helps us to visualise them as the sea. ☐

It helps us to visualise them as pieces that connect. ☐

1

Marks

Questions 31–40 are about *Mary the evacuee* on page **34**.

31. What year is the story set in?

_____

_____

1

32.

> ...many children were being **evacuated** to the countryside...

What does the word *evacuated* mean?

_____

_____

1

33. Why were the children being evacuated?

_____

1

34.

> ...mothers with **hankies** to wipe their tears away

Why has the author used the word *hankies* instead of *tissues*?

Tick one.

It is old-fashioned. ☐

It is funny. ☐

It is modern. ☐

It is cute. ☐

Marks

1

35. Why was Mary frightened? Give **two** reasons from the text.

1. _____

2. _____

2

36. How did Mary travel to the countryside?

_____

_____

1

37. How do you think Janet was feeling when Mary sat down next to her? What evidence is there for this?

_____

_____

2

SCHOLASTIC National Curriculum SATs Tests

Marks

38. How do you think Mary's mother might have been feeling as Mary climbed onto the train? Explain why.

_____

_____

2

39.

> They smiled when they saw **real** cows in a field for the first time!

What does the word _real_ mean in this sentence?

_____

1

40. What do you think will happen to Mary and Janet in the hall? Explain your answer.

_____

_____

_____

2

End of test

Test B Marks

Question	Focus	Possible marks	Actual marks
1	Information/key details	1	
2	Identifying/explaining choices of words and phrases	1	
3	Information/key details	1	
4	Information/key details	2	
5	Making inferences	1	
6	Making inferences	1	
7	Meanings of words	1	
8	Identifying/explaining choices of words and phrases	1	
9	Information/key details	1	
10	Information/key details	1	
11	Making inferences	1	
12	Meanings of words	1	
13	Identifying/explaining how information is related	1	
14	Information/key details	1	
15	Summarise	1	
16	Identifying/explaining how information is related	1	
17	Identifying/explaining how information is related	1	
18	Predicting	2	
19	Making inferences	2	
20	Making inferences	3	
21	Information/key details	1	
22	Meanings of words	1	
23	Making inferences	1	
24	Information/key details	1	
25	Information/key details	1	
26	Meanings of words	1	
27	Information/key details	2	
28	Information/key details	1	
29	Information/key details	1	
30	Identifying/explaining choices of words and phrases	1	
31	Information/key details	1	
32	Meanings of words	1	
33	Information/key details	1	
34	Identifying/explaining choices of words and phrases	1	
35	Making inferences	2	
36	Information/key details	1	
37	Making inferences	2	
38	Making inferences	2	
39	Meanings of words	1	
40	Predicting	2	
	Total	**50**	

Test C

Cleaning your teeth

Brush them twice a day,
That's what the dentists say.
To keep your teeth healthy and your gums too,
Brushing well is what you must do.

Up and down, forwards and back, side to side,
Get those bits of food that hide.
Clean off bacteria, clean off plaque,
Protect your teeth from a nasty attack.

For teeth that are very straight indeed,
Braces on them you might need.
Keep tooth enamel shining white,
For a super smile that's clean and bright.

Brush your teeth and tongue as well,
For breath that's fresh and sweet to smell.
Use toothpaste, just a pea-sized smear,
Then at the dentist's, have no fear!

A toothpaste blob upon your brush,
Take your time, no need to rush.
Say NO to gum disease and tooth decay,
Remember to brush them twice a day.

SCHOLASTIC National Curriculum SATs Tests

Vegetable pasta bake

This pasta bake is a quick, easy and delicious meal to cook. Originally from Italy, pasta comes in many different shapes and sizes such as spaghetti (long thin strips) and penne (short tubes). You can make your own pasta or buy fresh or dried pasta. This recipe can be made with homemade, dried or fresh pasta. You can also choose which shaped pasta you would like to use, although it works particularly well with penne.

Method

1. Pre-heat the oven to 200°C/gas mark 6.

2. Place all the vegetables in a baking tray and drizzle over the olive oil.

3. Roast the vegetables in the oven for approximately 30 minutes.

4. Meanwhile, boil the pasta for 5–6 minutes until just beginning to soften.

5. Remove the pasta from the heat and drain in a colander.

6. Once the vegetables are roasted, pour half the vegetables into a blender and blend into a smooth paste.

7. In a large bowl, mix the rest of the vegetables with the pasta, chopped tomatoes, garlic, basil and semi-cooked pasta.

8. Put the mixture into a baking dish and sprinkle over the grated cheese.

9. Turn the oven down to 170°C/gas mark 4

10. Bake the pasta for 40 minutes or until golden brown on top.

11. Serve with a cool, crisp, crunchy salad and enjoy your truly tasty vegetable pasta bake.

Ingredients

200g closed-cup mushrooms, chopped in half

1 red pepper, de-seeded and cut into quarters

1 green pepper, de-seeded and cut into quarters

2 small red onions, roughly chopped

2 small courgettes, thickly sliced

5 tablespoons of olive oil

6 large basil leaves, shredded

3 cloves of garlic, crushed

400g tomatoes, chopped

100g cheddar cheese, grated

400g penne pasta

All about your teeth

We use our teeth to chew and eat our food every day. Everyone's teeth are different and special to them, just like their fingerprints. Find out here about the different types of teeth, what teeth are made from and how to look after your teeth.

Different types of teeth

There are four different types of teeth: **incisors**, **canines**, **pre-molars** and **molars**. Molars are the big teeth at the back of your mouth and they are good at crushing food. Canines are for tearing and ripping food. Animals such as lions and tigers, which are hunters, have large canines. Incisors are the teeth at the front of your mouth that are used to bite into food.

How many teeth?

You have two sets of teeth during your lifetime. Your first set of teeth, which are often called baby teeth or milk teeth, grow when you are a baby and then start falling out to make space for your second set when you are about six years old. You have approximately 20 milk teeth. Adults can have up to 32 adult teeth. Sometimes adult teeth are called permanent teeth because these are your final set of teeth, which should last for the rest of your life.

What are teeth made from?

Some of your tooth is below the gum. This is called the **root**. The part of your tooth you can see is called the **crown**. The white layer on the outside of your tooth is **enamel**. This is hard and protects your tooth. Underneath the enamel is a layer called **dentine**, and in the centre of your tooth is **pulp**. Pulp is the living part of your tooth and is sensitive.

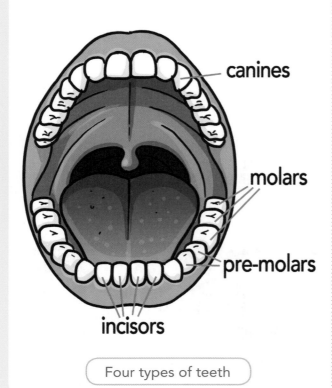

Four types of teeth

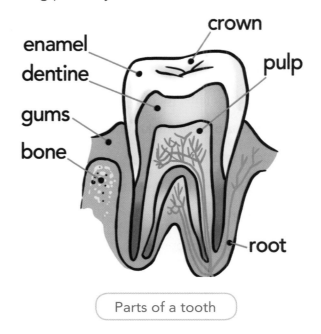

Parts of a tooth

SCHOLASTIC National Curriculum SATs Tests

What causes gum disease and tooth decay?

Plaque is a type of bacteria which forms when sugar is left on your teeth from sugary foods. The plaque and bacteria in your mouth can cause tooth decay and gum disease if you do not look after your teeth properly.

Looking after your teeth

Brushing your teeth, eating healthily and visiting the dentist all help to keep your teeth healthy and clean.

You should brush your teeth twice a day for at least two minutes. You can use a small sand-timer (usually available from the dentist) to check you are cleaning your teeth for long enough. Brushing your teeth can protect them from plaque. You should use a soft-bristled brush and a pea-sized blob of fluoride toothpaste to clean your teeth. It is important to make sure you clean *all* the surfaces of your teeth, and your tongue too.

Healthy eating can also help to care for your teeth. Calcium found in foods such as milk and cheese can help your teeth to grow strong. However, sugary foods such as sweets or fizzy drinks are bad for your teeth and should only be eaten as a special treat.

Going to the dentist regularly (every six months) can also help to look after your teeth. The dentist will look at your teeth to check that they are all in good health and there are no holes caused by plaque and other bacteria. Sometimes the dentist might give your teeth an extra special clean.

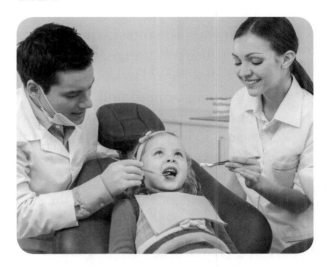

Making teeth straighter

Sometimes teeth do not grow straight. An orthodontist is a special dentist who straightens people's teeth. An orthodontist may suggest that you wear braces on your teeth for a short time. Braces are used to straighten teeth and come in many different types. Some braces can be taken in and out, while others are fixed to your teeth.

The duck rescue

Jackson was on his way home from swimming club. He was really hungry after training so he hoped Dad would have his dinner ready. It was only a short walk from the swimming pool across the park to his house. Jackson was just crossing the bridge over the stream when he heard a strange and scary noise on the path down below him. He stopped to listen. Something was flapping around and thumping its feet on the ground. Jackson wondered what to do. It was getting late and it was quite dark under the bridge, but something sounded like it might be in trouble. He decided to take a look and walked down the steps. Cautiously, he peered around the stone wall.

There, under the bridge, was a duck! It had a piece of plastic trapped around its beak. Jackson had learned at school how litter can harm wildlife just like this. The poor bird flapped its wings and stamped its webbed feet up and down. Its beautiful feathers were all over the path and it looked really thin. Jackson slowly tried to get closer to the bird. If only it would stand still, then he could untangle the plastic. But the bird flapped its wings even faster and dived into the water. Jackson watched the duck struggle to the other side of the stream, where it began rubbing its beak on a tree. Jackson looked around the park to see if there was anyone who could help. But it was empty. Everyone had gone home.

Jackson put down his swimming bag and rummaged around inside. Somewhere under his wet towel and swimming shorts was his mobile phone. Luckily he found it, but there wasn't much time as his phone was flashing to tell him the battery was low. He quickly did a search to find the phone number for the animal rescue centre and dialled the number. The animal rescue team were really helpful. They asked Jackson to describe the duck and give them directions. Then they told him to stay at a safe distance from the duck but where he could still see it, and they would be there as quickly as they could.

SCHOLASTIC National Curriculum SATs Tests

After that, Jackson phoned his dad to let him know where he was. He then sat down on a nearby park bench. He watched the duck waddle up and down the path by the stream. Jackson began to shiver. He pulled his hoody up over his head and plunged his hands deep into his pockets to keep warm.

First to arrive was Jackson's dad, carrying a flask of warm tea and a packet of biscuits to share. Together they sat on the bench and kept an eye on the struggling duck. It felt like they were waiting forever but in fact it was only fifteen minutes. Finally, the animal rescue team arrived.

"It's over there," Jackson told the rescue workers, pointing at the duck on the other side of the stream.

Steadily, the workers crept closer to the duck, holding out bird seed on their hands to show they were friendly. The duck tried to get away again but the rescue team managed to catch it and gently pull off the plastic. They were wearing thick gloves to protect their hands from any pecking. The duck gobbled up the bird seed. Jackson knew how the duck felt: *his* tummy was rumbling too!

The animal rescue team decided to take the duck back to the centre because it was so weak and had damaged its wing with all the flapping around. They thanked Jackson for saving the bird and, as they loaded the duck into the van, they told him he was a real hero.

"You should be on the front page of the newspaper. 'Local hero rescues wildlife', it would say! I wouldn't be surprised if the newspaper rang and asked to take your photograph," one of the rescue workers suggested to Jackson, smiling.

The next day, Jackson got a phone call from the local newspaper to ask…

Marks

> **Questions** 1–8 are about *Cleaning your teeth* on page **50**.

1. In the first line of the poem, what does *them* mean?

Tick **one**.

Children ☐

Dentists ☐

People ☐

Teeth ☐

1

2. a. How often does the text say to brush your teeth?

_____

1

b. According to the text, who says so?

_____

1

SCHOLASTIC National Curriculum SATs Tests

3. Which word in the text rhymes with *plaque*?

_____

4. What does the text say you might need for straight teeth?

_____

5. What does the text tell you to do to your tongue?

_____

Marks

1

1

1

6. What **two** words does the author use to describe how you might want your breath to smell?

1. _____

2. _____

7. Circle the word in the text that rhymes with *brush*.

hush   rush   blush   crush

8. What might happen if you don't brush your teeth twice a day?

_____

■SCHOLASTIC National Curriculum SATs Tests

Marks

Questions 9–20 are about *Vegetable pasta bake* on page **51**.

9. Which country does pasta originally come from?

_____

_____

1

10. What does the author say to encourage the reader to make the vegetable pasta bake? Give **two** different reasons from the text.

1._____

2._____

_____

2

11. What type of pasta does the recipe recommend for this dish?

_____

1

Marks

12. How should the mushrooms be prepared for cooking?

Tick **one**.

Chopped ☐

Grated ☐

Shredded ☐

Sliced ☐

1

13.

> ● 2 **small** red onions, roughly chopped
>
> ● 2 **small** courgettes, thickly sliced

The author has used the word *small* twice. Suggest another word with the same meaning that could be used instead.

_____

1

Marks

14. How should the onions be chopped in this recipe?

Tick **one**.

Roughly ☐

Finely ☐

Thickly ☐

Quickly ☐

1

15. How many tablespoons of olive oil are needed in the recipe?

_____

1

16. How many grams (g) of grated cheese are needed in the recipe?

_____

1

17. In the method, why are the steps numbered?

_____

1

Marks

18. What temperature should the oven be pre-heated to?

_____

_____

1

19.

> *Roast the vegetables in the oven for **approximately** 30 minutes.*

What does the word *approximately* mean in this sentence?

_____

_____

1

20. Tick **true** or **false** in the following table to show what you should do when making a vegetable pasta bake.

	True	False
Roast the vegetables in the oven for 5–6 minutes.		
Drain the pasta in a colander.		
Blend all of the vegetables in a blender.		
Sprinkle grated cheese over the baking dish.		

1

Marks

Questions 21–33 are about *All about your teeth* on pages **52–53**.

21. What do we use our teeth for every day?

_____

1

22. Draw lines to match the teeth with their jobs.

Canines		Good at crushing food.

Molars		Used to bite into food.

Incisors		For tearing and ripping food.

1

23. What type of animals have large canines?

_____

1

24. **Find** and **copy** the title of the paragraph that tells you the number of teeth we have.

_____

Marks

1

25. Why do you think humans have baby teeth and adult teeth? Give a reason for your answer.

_____

_____

2

26. Circle **one**. Adult teeth are sometimes called your:

permanent teeth.   premature teeth.

temporary teeth.   established teeth.

1

27. What is enamel?

Tick **one**.

Tooth that is below the gum ☐

The white layer on the outside of your tooth ☐

The toothpaste you use ☐

The centre of your tooth ☐

1

28. Why do you think the words *root*, *crown*, *enamel*, *dentine* and *pulp* are in bold writing in the main text?

Tick **one**.

To make the key words stand out ☐

To look smart ☐

To act as a subheading ☐

To add variety to the paragraph ☐

29. Why are sugary foods bad for your teeth? Use evidence from the text to explain your answer.

_____

_____

_____

_____

30. What **three** things can you do to look after your teeth?

1. _____

2. _____

3. _____

31.

> *Brushing your teeth can **protect** them from plaque.*

What does the word *protect* mean?

_____

1

32.

> *It is important to make sure you clean **all** the surfaces of your teeth, and your tongue too.*

Why do you think the word *all* is in italics in the text?

_____

1

33. What is an orthodontist?

Tick **one**.

A dentist who cleans teeth ☐

A dentist who straightens teeth ☐

A dentist's patient ☐

A doctor who removes teeth ☐

1

SCHOLASTIC National Curriculum SATs Tests

Marks

Questions 34–38 are about *The duck rescue* on pages 54–55.

34. Number these events (1–5) to show the order in which they take place. The first one has been done for you.

Finally, the animal rescue team arrived.	
There, under the bridge, was a duck!	
First to arrive was Jackson's dad.	
Jackson was on his way home from swimming club.	I
He did a search... for the animal rescue centre and dialled the number.	

1

35. Give **two** examples that show Jackson was cold.

1. _____

2. _____

2

36. What clues are there in the text to suggest that the duck might be hungry? List **two**.

1. _____

2. _____

2

37.

> *There, under the bridge, was a **duck**!*

a. The word *duck* has two meanings. Tick the correct meaning in this context.

To lower your head or bend down ☐

A type of bird ☐

Marks

1

b. Explain how the reader knows which meaning the word has in this context. Give **two** reasons.

_____

_____

2

38.

> *The next day, Jackson got a phone call from the local newspaper to ask...*

Why might the newspaper have been phoning Jackson? How is this suggested in the text?

_____

_____

2

End of test

SCHOLASTIC National Curriculum SATs Tests

Question	Focus	Possible marks	Actual marks
1	Meanings of words	1	
2	Information/key details	2	
3	Identifying/explaining choice of words and phrases	1	
4	Information/key details	1	
5	Information/key details	1	
6	Identifying/explaining choice of words and phrases	1	
7	Identifying/explaining choice of words and phrases	1	
8	Predicting	1	
9	Information/key details	1	
10	Making inferences	2	
11	Information/key details	1	
12	Information/key details	1	
13	Meanings of words	1	
14	Information/key details	1	
15	Information/key details	1	
16	Information/key details	1	
17	Identifying/explaining how information is related	1	
18	Information/key details	1	
19	Meanings of words	1	
20	Information/key details	1	
21	Information/key details	1	
22	Information/key details	1	
23	Information/key details	1	
24	Identifying/explaining how information is related	1	
25	Making inferences	2	
26	Identifying/explaining how information is related	1	
27	Information/key details	1	
28	Identifying/explaining how information is related	1	
29	Information/key details	3	
30	Information/key details	3	
31	Meanings of words	1	
32	Identifying/explaining how information is related	1	
33	Information/key details	1	
34	Summarise	1	
35	Making inferences	2	
36	Making inferences	2	
37	Meanings of words	3	
38	Making inferences	2	
	Total	50	

Marking and assessing the papers

The mark schemes provide detailed examples of correct answers (although other variations/ phrasings are often acceptable) and an explanation about what the answer should contain to be awarded a mark or marks.

Although the mark scheme sometimes contains alternative suggestions for correct answers, some children may find other ways of expressing a correct answer. When marking these tests, exercise judgement when assessing the accuracy or relevance of an answer and give credit for correct responses.

Marks table

At the end of each test there is a table for you to insert the number of marks achieved for each question. This will enable you to see which areas your child needs to practise further.

National standard in Reading

The mark that your child gets in the test paper will be known as the 'raw score' (for example, '22' in 22/50). The raw score will be converted to a scaled score and children achieving a scaled score of 100 or more will achieve the national standard in that subject. These 'scaled scores' enable results to be reported consistently year-on-year.

The guidance in the table below shows the marks that children need to achieve to reach the national standard. This should be treated as a guide only, as the number of marks may vary. You can also find up-to-date information about scaled scores on our website: www.scholastic.co.uk/nationaltests

Marks achieved	Standard
0–27	Has not met the national standard in Reading for Year 4
28–50	Has met the national standard in Reading for Year 4

Mark scheme for Test A (pages 7–27)

Q	Answers	Marks
1	**Award 2 marks** for: A satellite is going to Mars. The satellite will explore the surface of Mars. **Award 1 mark** for either of the above.	2
2	**Award 1 mark** for scientists	1
3	**Award 1 mark** for digital	1
4	**Award 2 marks** for Colour: Red and Cause: Rust **Award 1 mark** for either of the above.	2
5	**Award 1 mark** for more	1
6	**Award 2 marks** for any **two** of the following: ● To investigate the planet Mars ● To answer scientists' questions ● To take photographs ● To find out more/to explore the planet Mars **Award 1 mark** for each correct reason.	2
7	**Award 1 mark** for: Journey	1
8	**Award 1 mark** for any answer that suggests: Appropriate/right/correct	1
9	**Award 1 mark** for: So you don't scare the birds.	1
10	**Award 1 mark** for: To help you see the birds more clearly.	1
11	**Award 1 mark** for: So the birds don't see them.	1
12	**Award 1 mark** for: keep a chart	1
13	**Award 1 mark** for pigeons	1
14	**Award 1 mark** for two	1
15	**Award 1 mark** for: Blue tit	1
16	**Award 1 mark** for: Robin	1
17	**Award 1 mark** for brown	1
18	**Award 1 mark** for seeds and nuts	1
19	Blackbird → Gardens and parks Blue tits → In the trees Sparrows → Towns and cities	1
20	**Award 1 mark** for answers that suggest any of the following: snow or ice hiding food sources, the ground becomes too hard for them to find seeds or insects in it, many trees and plants lose their leaves and fruit in the winter.	1
21	**Award 1 mark** for: A piece of string	1
22	**Award 1 mark** for 400	1
23	**Award 1 mark** for: To encourage the reader to make a bird cake.	1

Q	Answers	Marks
24	**a. Award I mark** for any answer that suggests: To make a hole/stab/cut. **b. Award 2 marks** for an answer such as: with care and an explanation that implies: you need to avoid hurting yourself/you could break the pot. **Award I mark** for an understanding of *carefully* but with no explanation.	1 2
25	**Award I mark** for any one of the following: ● In a tree/bush ● On a branch ● In the garden/school grounds	1
26	**a. Award I mark** for salted (nuts)/(nuts) with salt **b. Award I mark** for: They would make the birds ill.	1 1
27	**Award I mark** for humans	1
28	**Award I mark** for: He is idle.	1
29	**Award I mark** for under a tree/in the shade of a tree/in the forest	1
30	**Award I mark** for food	1
31	**Award 3 marks** for any valid feeling, such as scared/frightened/upset/terrified and three pieces of evidence from the text such as: ● She trembled. ● She cried/a tear rolled down her cheek. ● Her (long) whiskers quivered. **Award 2 marks** for a feeling and two pieces of evidence. **Award I mark** for a feeling and one piece of evidence.	3
32	**Award I mark** for any answer that suggests: shouted/roared/yelled.	1
33	**Award I mark** for: He thought she was funny.	1
34	**Award 2 marks** for any one valid explanation, such as: ● She didn't want the lion to change his mind and eat her. ● She wanted to get away quickly. She was clever [with a suitable reason/explanation]. **Award I mark** for a statement such as 'The mouse was clever' but with no reason/explanation given.	2
35	**Award I mark** for Clearing leaves from the path	1
36	**Award 2 marks** for any two valid explanations, such as: ● She was scared of the lion/The lion was frightening. ● She didn't know if he would eat her (this time). ● She didn't know why he was roaring. **Award I mark** for one of the above.	2
37	**Award I mark** for any valid feeling, such as: scared/frightened/embarrassed.	1
38	**Award 2 marks** for any answer that suggests the following: ● She had been able to help/was proud to have helped the lion. ● She had proved the lion wrong. **Award I mark** for one of the above.	2
39	**Award I mark** for any answer that suggests: Small creatures can be helpful/important/useful too.	1

Mark scheme for Test B (pages 28–48)

Q	Answers	Marks
1	**Award 1 mark** for They are watching the lion and/or They are looking tense.	1
2	**Award 1 mark** for tense	1
3	**Award 1 mark** for any one of the following: ● By the fence ● In a cage ● At the zoo	1
4	**a. Award 1 mark** for knife-sharp or sharp **b. Award 1 mark** for powerful	1 1
5	**Award 1 mark** for any answer that suggests: It is really loud/a horrible sound.	1
6	**Award 1 mark** for any answer that gives a valid reason, such as one of the following: ● They are buzzing around. ● They are tickling him. ● They keep landing on him.	1
7	**Award 1 mark** for any answer that suggests: super/wonderful/fantastic/impressive/splendid/glorious/special/great	1
8	**Award 1 mark** for any answer that suggests: It gives the poem a repeating pattern and sound/makes the poem flow/makes the poem memorable.	1
9	**Award 1 mark** for: to Grandma's house	1
10	**Award 1 mark** for: to pick bluebells/flowers (for Grandma)	1
11	**Award 1 mark** for any answer that suggests one of the following: ● He thinks he is going to eat Little Red Riding Hood (and Grandma) (for lunch). ● He is pleased with himself (for being so clever).	1
12	**Award 1 mark** for: Grandma's clothes.	1
13	**Award 1 mark** for: To show that Little Red Riding Hood is shouting	1
14	**Award 1 mark** for the woodcutter	1
15	**Award 1 mark** for	1

The woodcutter rescues Little Red Riding Hood from the Big Bad Wolf.	5
The Big Bad Wolf talks to Little Red Riding Hood in the woods.	3
The Big Bad Wolf dresses in Grandma's clothes.	4
Little Red Riding Hood is asked to take a basket of cakes and fruit to Grandma's house.	1
Little Red Riding Hood leaves the path to pick bluebells.	2

Q	Answers	Marks
16	**Award 1 mark** for **a.** stage directions and **c.** dialogue	1
17	**Award 1 mark** for: To tell the actors what to do	1
18	**Award 2 marks** for answers that suggest: they have tea and cake/eat the cakes in the basket (together) with an explanation: Grandma says so/invites the woodcutter to stay for tea and cake. **Award 1 mark** if only one part is given correctly.	2
19	**Award 2 marks** for any two of the following: ● She says 'I love visiting Grandma'. ● She takes Grandma a basket of cakes and fruit. ● She picks bluebells because she thinks they will cheer Grandma up. ● She is excited to see Grandma when she comes out of the cupboard. ● She gives Grandma a hug. **Award 1 mark** for each correct reason.	2
20	**Award 3 marks** for three character qualities such as helpful, naughty, silly, loving, kind, friendly, using evidence from the text. For example: ● Little Red Riding Hood is helpful because she takes the cakes to Grandma for her mother. ● Little Red Riding Hood is naughty because she spoke to a stranger in the wood. **Award 2 marks** for two qualities/reasons. **Award 1 mark** for one quality/reason.	3
21	**Award 1 mark** for: Along the Earth's plate edges	1
22	**Award 1 mark** for any answer suggesting that the magma comes through the Earth's surface at speed, such as: Blasts through, bursts through, bursts out, flows out, comes out quickly	1
23	**Award 1 mark** for answers that suggest that mountains are created from lava hardening on the Earth.	1
24	**Award 1 mark** for three	1
25	**Award 1 mark** for: A volcano that has not erupted within the last 10,000 years but could erupt again	1
26	**Award 1 mark** for any answer that suggests: disastrous/terrible/awful/catastrophic/upsetting	1
27	**Award 2 marks** for any two of the following: ● The soil is very rich. ● Crops grow extremely well. ● Tourists come to see volcanoes. ● Create jobs for people living there. **Award 1 mark** for one of the above.	2
28	**Award 1 mark** for: Molten rock from deep inside the Earth	1
29	**Award 1 mark** for: Tiny pieces of rocks and minerals thrown from the volcano	1

Q	Answers	Marks
30	**Award 1 mark** for: It helps us to visualise them as pieces that connect.	1
31	**Award 1 mark** for 1940	1
32	**Award 1 mark** for any answer that suggests: moved away/transported to a different place/re-homed/taken away	1
33	**Award 1 mark** for any answer that suggests one of the following: ● For their safety/to keep them safe/because it was safer in the countryside ● Because London was being bombed	1
34	**Award 1 mark** for: It is old-fashioned.	1
35	**Award 2 marks** for any two of the following: ● She would miss her mother. ● She was on her own. ● She had not been to the countryside before. **Award 1 mark** for one correct reason.	2
36	**Award 1 mark** for By train	1
37	**Award 2 marks** for any answer that suggests: Upset/sad/unhappy/frightened/scared because she was crying. **Award 1 mark** for either part correct.	2
38	**Award 2 marks** for any suitable feeling and reason given, such as: ● Her mother was feeling sad/upset because she was going to miss Mary/ because Mary was going away. ● Her mother was feeling relieved/happy because her daughter was going to be safe and away from the bombs. **Award 1 mark** for a suitable feeling or reason.	2
39	**Award 1 mark** for any answer that implies the word real means actual/live/ living/not pretend/not toys or pictures.	1
40	**Award 2 marks** for explanations that include reference to them being given a new home to live in because Mary wondered what her 'new home' would be like and her mother wanted her to make a good 'first impression'. **Award 1 mark** for an answer that makes reference to being given a new home but provides no explanation.	2

Q	Answers	Marks
1	**Award 1 mark** for: Teeth	1
2	**a. Award 1 mark** for twice a day **b. Award 1 mark** for dentists	1 1
3	**Award 1 mark** for attack	1
4	**Award 1 mark** for braces	1
5	**Award 1 mark** for brush it	1
6	**Award 1 mark** for fresh, sweet	1
7	**Award 1 mark** for: rush.	1
8	**Award 1 mark** for any answer that suggests: you might get gum disease or tooth decay.	1
9	**Award 1 mark** for Italy	1
10	**Award 2 marks** for both: ● Quick and easy (to make) ● Delicious/truly tasty **Award 1 mark** for each correct reason.	2
11	**Award 1 mark** for penne (or tubes)	1
12	**Award 1 mark** for: Chopped	1
13	**Award 1 mark** for any other word that means 'small', such as: little/tiny/mini	1
14	**Award 1 mark** for: Roughly	1
15	**Award 1 mark** for 5	1
16	**Award 1 mark** for 100	1
17	**Award 1 mark** for any answer that suggests: To show the order they must be completed in.	1
18	**Award 1 mark** for 200°C and/or gas mark 6	1
19	**Award 1 mark** for any answer that suggests: roughly/around/about	1
20	**Award 1 mark** for	1

	True	False
Roast the vegetables in the oven for 5–6 minutes.		✓
Drain the pasta in a colander.	✓	
Blend all of the vegetables in a blender.		✓
Sprinkle grated cheese over the baking dish.	✓	

Q	Answers	Marks
21	**Award 1 mark** for chew and eat food	1

Q	Answers	Marks
22	Canines → Used to bite into food. Molars → Good at crushing food. Incisors → For tearing and ripping food.	1
23	**Award 1 mark** for hunters	1
24	**Award 1 mark** for How many teeth?	1
25	**Award 2 marks** for answers that indicate size and give a reason, for example: Teeth do not grow but a human does, so the second set of teeth are bigger to fit in your mouth or that adult teeth would be too big for a baby's mouth. **Award 1 mark** for answers that indicate size but do not give a reason.	2
26	**Award 1 mark** for: permanent teeth.	1
27	**Award 1 mark** for: The white layer on the outside of your tooth	1
28	**Award 1 mark** for: To make the key words stand out	1
29	**Award 3 marks** for an answer that explains: • Sugary foods leave sugar on your teeth. • When sugar is left on your teeth it causes plaque (to form/grow). • Plaque can cause tooth decay (and gum disease). **Award 2 marks** for an answer that explains two of the above. **Award 1 mark** for an answer that explains one of the above.	3
30	**Award 3 marks** for all three correct. • Brush your teeth twice a day • Eat healthily • Go to the dentist (regularly) **Award 2 marks** for two correct. **Award 1 mark** for one correct.	3
31	**Award 1 mark** for any answer that suggests: defend/guard/safeguard/stop damage or harm	1
32	**Award 1 mark** for any answer that suggests: to highlight/emphasise the importance of the word *all*	1
33	**Award 1 mark** for: A dentist who straightens teeth	1
34	**Award 1 mark** for	1

Finally, the animal rescue team arrived.	5
There under the bridge was a duck!	2
First was arrive was Jackson's dad.	4
Jackson was on his way home from swimming club.	1
He did a search... for the animal rescue centre and dialled the number.	3

Q	Answers	Marks
35	**Award 2 marks** for any two valid examples, such as: • He began to shiver. • He pulled his hoody up (to keep warm). • He put his hands in his pockets (to keep warm). • He wanted to keep warm. **Award 1 mark** for one correct example.	2
36	**Award 2 marks** for any two of the following: • It gobbled/ate fast/ate the bird seed. • Its beak was trapped. • It looked really thin. • It was weak. **Award 1 mark** for one correct example.	2
37	**a. Award 1 mark** for: A type of bird **b. Award 2 marks** for any two valid explanations, such as: • Because the word is used as a noun • Because it is a thing/object • Because it is not a verb/action • Because the author describes the duck • Because it has a beak **Award 1 mark** for one valid explanation.	1 2
38	**Award 2 marks** for: • To ask to take Jackson's photograph. • One of the rescue workers suggested it. **Award 1 mark** for either of the above.	2

■SCHOLASTIC National Curriculum SATs Tests

QUICK TESTS FOR SATs SUCCESS

BOOST YOUR CHILD'S CONFIDENCE WITH 10-MINUTE SATs TESTS

- Bite-size mini SATs tests which take just 10 minutes to complete
- Covers key National Test topics
- Full answers and progress chart provided to track improvement
- Available for Years 1 to 6

Find out more at www.scholastic.co.uk